The Mill Grinds Fine

"Helen Alderfer, long known to me
as an elegant and early female editor at the Mennonite
Publishing House, reveals in this volume the saving grace of
poetry. At any age, poets write to retain and redeem memory, but
perhaps even more so in what Helen calls 'the winter years.' From
that vantage point, she writes with wisdom and generosity, in love
with life yet mindful of loss. Family, place, faith, and imagination
are the topics of these poems, which reach back to the
nineteenth century and stand carefully articulated
and lovingly framed for the future."

—Julia Kasdorf, Author, *Sleeping Preacher*

The Mill Grinds Fine

Collected Poems

Helen Wade Alderfer

Helen W. Alderfer

DreamSeeker Books
TELFORD, PENNSYLVANIA

an imprint of
Cascadia Publishing House LLC

Copublished with
Herald Press
Scottdale, Pennsylvania

Cascadia Publishing House orders, information, reprint permissions:
contact@CascadiaPublishingHouse.com
1-215-723-9125
126 Klingerman Road, Telford PA 18969
www.CascadiaPublishingHouse.com

The Mill Grinds Fine
Copyright © 2009 by Cascadia Publishing House, Telford, PA 18969
All rights reserved
DreamSeeker Books is an imprint of Cascadia Publishing House LLC
Copublished with Herald Press, Scottdale, PA
Library of Congress Catalog Number: 2008042255
ISBN 13: 978-1-931038-60-7; ISBN 10: 1-931038-60-0
Book design by Cascadia Publishing House
Cover design by Gwen M. Stamm
Illustrations, including cover background,
by Rodney C. Summer
Author photo by Tyler Klassen, used by permission of the *Goshen News*

The paper used in this publication is recycled and meets the
minimum requirements of American National Standard for Information
Sciences—Permanence of Paper for Printed Library Materials, ANSI Z39.48-1984.1984

"The Bouquets," "On the Birth of Greta," "Senescence," and "Quaker Meeting" appeared in *Purpose Magazine*.
"Missing in Action" appeared in *Gospel Herald*.
"White Is Winter's Way" appeared in *Christian Monitor*.
"Transformation Mennonites USA," The Wedding Day," and "Old Age" appeared in *The Mennonite*. "Two Greyhounds in New York City" appeared in *Greyhound Review*.

Library of Congress Cataloguing-in-Publication Data
Alderfer, Helen Wade.
 The mill grinds fine : collected poems / Helen Wade Alderfer.
  p. cm.
 ISBN-13: 978-1-931038-60-7 (trade pbk. : alk. paper)
 ISBN-10: 1-931038-60-0 (trade pbk. : alk. paper)
 1. Mennonite women--Poetry. I. Title.
 PS3601.L3457M55 2009
 811'.6--dc22
                    2008042255

15 14 13 12 11 10 09 08   10 9 8 7 6 5 4 3 2 1

*Dedicated with heartfelt gratitude
to my husband Edwin Stover Alderfer
and to our children Eric, Ann, Faith, Mary, Amy*

To Rhoda —
I appreciate your friendship,
your poetry and your
thoughtful transportation.

— Helen W. Alderfer

Contents

About the Poet   11
The Mill Grinds Fine   12

Childhood
Childhood • 15
We Had Dick • 16
Verena Graber Conrad (1846-1930) • 17
Living Toward Sunday • 18
After Church • 19
The Second Chocolate • 20
Easter Finery Was Verboten • 21
Pride • 22
Remember Who You Are • 23
The Choice • 24
School Was Important • 25
Mother Read to Us • 26
Our Watkins Man • 27
What Did Mother Fear? • 28
Mother Fed Tramps • 29
What Did the Preacher Say? • 30
Lost Stories • 31

Parents
The Mystery of Ancestors • 35
Mother Was Generous • 36
Mother Found a Way • 37
Mother Was Strong • 38
The Topic • 39
Mother and Norman Vincent Peale • 40
Our Mother the Writer • 41

Neither Snow Nor Rain Nor Sleet. . . . • 42
Sunsets • 43
Mother and the Car • 44
Mother's Wool Comforters • 46
Waiting for Summer • 47
Our Family Did Not Burn Corn • 48
Shared Loneliness • 49
The Brown Suit • 50
September 28 • 51
The Loser at the County Fair • 52
Dream—June 2005 • 53

Gardens

Good Work • 57
The Forager • 58
Can We Share a Garden? • 59
The Bouquets • 60
Remembering • 61
I Need a Letter from Home • 62
Simone Barbadillo's Garden • 63
A Bitter End • 64
Our Summer Pheasant • 65
Calendar Garden • 66
Winter's Way • 67

Remembered

The Two-Cent Copper Coin • 71
The Schoolhouse Walk • 72
Miss Coney • 73
Rayma Rawson • 74

Memory • 75
The Flamboyant Tree • 76
Going Home • 77
Quaker Meeting • 78
The Happy Hour • 79
The Bird Nest • 80
The Night Blooming Cereus • 81
The Gift • 82
Carver School—Room 37 • 83
On the Birth of Granddaughter Greta • 84
Rejoice and Be Glad (for Elaine and Harold) • 85
Two Greyhounds in New York City • 86
The Trains Of My Life • 87
Counted Treasures Remain • 88
The Particulars of My Life • 89

Reflections

Waiting for a Poem • 93
Hymn to the Sun • 94
He Finds His Poem • 95
Liberation • 96
The Little Grapes • 97
October 28 • 98
The Happy Family • 99
He Cried, Too (A Friend's Story) • 100
Keys • 101
Moving • 102
Waiting for Tomorrow in Assisted Living • 103
Who Will Sing the Songs? • 104
Transformation Mennonites USA • 105

Questions • 106
Portent • 107

Husband
The Wedding Day • 111
August 12, 1944 • 112
Our Anniversaries • 113
2003 • 114
The Journey • 115
The Killdeer • 116
The Sorrows • 117
Tears • 118
The Giving Away • 119
Our Gardens • 120
Resurrection • 121

Mortality
Instructions to Adam and Eve • 125
They Also Lived • 126
Missing in Action • 127
Which Shade of Black? • 128
Emily's Secret • 129
The Leavetaking • 130
Summer Cannot Be Stayed • 131
Gathered Home • 132
Senescence • 133
Old Age • 134
Called Home • 135

About the Poet

Helen Wade Alderfer grew up near Sterling, Illinois. A life-long love of learning led Alderfer from a one-room school to an education degree from Goshen College in Goshen, Indiana, where she met and married Edwin S. Alderfer. While mothering five children, she taught school and worked as a writer, book reviewer, and retreat leader.

Alderfer was an editor of *Christian Living* for twenty-five years and of *On the Line* for fourteen years. She edited the book *A Farthing in Her Hand*. Her poems have been published in *Beams of Light, The Voice, Gospel Herald, Purpose, The Mennonite, On the Line, Christian Living*, and more. She lives and continues to write in Goshen, Indiana.

The Mill Grinds Fine

*With bits and pieces
of one short life, the mill grinds
true and very fine*

All of my experiences have been grist for the mill. Whatever life brought to me, I put between the stones, not knowing how fine the mill would grind.

The grain offered to my mill came from childhood, life with my husband and five children, making homes and gardens in seven states and countries, teaching, reading, editing and book reviewing, and leading retreats.

I wish I knew if I thought in poems before I could read or write. My first poem was published in *Beams of Light* when I was eight. I have written poems all my life, although there were desert years.

Many years ago I visited a Lancaster County woman, housebound in a farmhouse bedroom. When her sister was ill and she could not visit, she wrote a poem to her. "After that, everything came in poems," she said to me. At fifty, I did not have the imagination to understand how a woman could write her first poem in her eighties and then continue to write them. Now I know.

When my husband died, people offered many kind words. One person said, "You still have poetry." I thought it was a strange thing to say when I was not sure anything would help. But poetry *was* still there.

I enjoy reading and writing many forms of poetry. Poetry and my poetry writing group are important in my life today. I have come to see that birth and death are both mysteries. I honor the mystery that is here.

—*Helen Wade Alderfer*
 Goshen, Indiana

Childhood

Helen Verene Wade Alderfer 1919–

Summer

I remember the day
When our mother at last said,
"You can go barefoot."

Childhood

I would tell you of that childhood,
    the child, not a captive on an isolated farm,
    not lonely in the loneliness
    but a glad free spirit busy with happiness.
I would tell you of the riches God poured
    into the turning seasons,
    and I the beneficiary
    running to catch the smallest grains of glory.
I would tell you of the gift of years
    untouched by shadow.
I would tell you that the gold of those years
    has lit my life
    and I know will shine to the day I am called home.
It drives me to my knees.

12/19/04

We Had Dick

Dick was old and slow and bony but he was what we had.
We begged Mother for a pony but she said, "You have Dick."
Dick had pulled the buggy when Father courted Mother.
Dick brought Father seven miles to town to the lawyer's house
    where Mother kept house and cared for the invalid wife.
Those must have been hours of idyllic dreams
    for Mary and Clark.
The farm they would rent was run-down but
    Father would make it a fine place,
    maybe even a show place.
The house was old and decrepit but
    Mother would make it
    the house beautiful for their life together.
Dick carried the memory of those rides in his head.
So when he was too old to work he grazed the meadow
    and gave us children rides.
Our pleading never moved Mother.
Dick was destined for our childhood.
Some days I hated Dick.
One November morning Aunt Lena called us for school.
"Hurry," she said, "there is a surprise downstairs."
Please God, I begged, let it be the pony.
Dashing downstairs we found Grandmother
sitting on her low chair at the kitchen stove
holding a new baby—our brother.
At that moment we knew we would never get a pony.

10/24/98

Verena Graber Conrad (1846-1930)

Grandmother sat all day in the wicker rocker piecing quilts,
 intricate blue and white "Ocean Wave" quilts.
She hoped to make one for each of her
 fifteen granddaughters
 but died at age eighty-five, the goal unfulfilled.
She pitied girl babies and pitied me at my birth,
 saying life was hard for girls.
She knew of hardship—with ten children,
 an immigrant to the United States at forty-one,
 widowed at forty-four.
She wore Old Country clothes, the long dark tiny-print dress
 with two pockets,
 one for the small sack of numbers that told her
 which Psalm to read before she started work,
 the other for rock candy on a string for grandchildren.
She wore a head covering and a dark homespun apron.
Speaking French and a Swiss German dialect,
 she never learned English.

She sat small and shadow-like at the window.
Beyond it the Illinois prairie reached to the sky
 while she mourned the mountains of Switzerland.
Sundays I took sermon notes and brought them home to her.
Who knows what I brought. I only know it pleased her.
The notes ended, she offered me a piece of rock candy
 and patted my arm in dismissal.

I thought she was a woman whose footsteps
 I would never follow
 until years later when I tried to
 piece the intricate details of life into a whole.
I could not know that I would hold her memory
 on a slender thread sweet as rock candy.

Living Toward Sunday

At Sunday Service Mother sat straight,
    leaning slightly forward,
    following the Bible readings, taking sermon notes,
    singing lustily and kneeling devoutly.
For her the sermon was never boring,
    or the prayers too long.
Nothing distracted her focused attention.
I remember the hard bench,
    the cold linoleum floor when we knelt to pray.
I remember that the church was hot in summer,
    frigid in winter.
I longed for a squirrel frisking in the tree at the window,
    for a restless child's crying in the next bench.
Mother lived all week toward Sunday.
It was not my favorite day,
    yet I learned my first lesson in devotion sitting
    beside Mother in Sunday service.

1/98

After Church

After church and Sunday school
    my brother and I would hurry to the car
nosed into one of the stalls
    still there from horse and buggy days.
In the cool shade we waited for
    the rest of our family.
Mother was born one of God's social servants
    and talked long after church.
I know now that it was her oasis in the
    desert place of an isolated farm.
My brother and I bounced on the leather seats
    a sort of small trampoline.
We heard the sparrows chirping in the eaves
    the drone of voices from the church.
We waited and waited and waited,
    small practice for eternity.

The Second Chocolate

This was the Sunday before Christmas,
    the Sunday we would receive
        the little box of candy from the church.
We children huddled under the car blanket
    on the way to church,
        while visions of candy danced in our heads.
We knew there would be hard candy, crunchy pieces and
    one chocolate; dome-shaped, big, delicious,
        filled with something white. Years later,
        Godiva chocolates would never taste so good.
The windows of the car were frozen shut.
    Father peered through a small scraped spot
    and drove very slowly.
At home we emptied the candy boxes to assess our treasure.
I had two pieces of chocolate, definitely a mistake.
    My brother had one.
No, I would not trade a chocolate
    for several of his hard candies,
    nor would I share the second piece.
At the dinner table, lifting our heads in prayer,
    I saw my brother's pale eyes fixed on me.
He was wondering where I would hide my candy.
    I was wondering too where it might be safe.
After dinner my brother and I went outside to make a
    snowman, perhaps once in our lifetime, a snowwoman.
Then we came in cold and wet and checked our candy again.
We ate some of the hard pieces but not the chocolate.
I ate one with a Christmas tree design in the middle.
    My brother was whining with the injustice of his lot.
"Put them away," my mother ordered. Did we? If so, where?
God alone knows if that second chocolate spoiled Christmas.

12/25/00

Easter Finery Was Verboten

Mother believed that there should be
    no new clothes on Easter Sunday.
"Easter is not clothes," she said firmly.
So we wore our usual church clothes on Easter Sunday.
I don't recall if we felt self-righteous or ashamed.
We were taught that we were a peculiar people
    but I wondered, did we have to be that peculiar?
Many of Mother's teachings fell on deaf ears
    but some live on forever.
This Easter I put on a dress
    bought for a daughter's wedding seven years ago.
Brightly flowered, it looked almost new and I wondered
    if it might pass as Easter finery.
But I thought I heard Mother say, "It's all right, Helenalie.
    Go ahead, wear it.
    You don't have to feel guilty over this one."

5/23/98

Pride

Mother believed "Pride goes before a fall."
The word 'proud' was not used in the church papers.
My sister and I asked Mother, "Don't you think that
    we are a little pretty?"
But she would not say it for fear we would become proud.
And yet without saying it I knew that
    Mother was proud of her children,
We had a good name in the neighborhood.
We stood for something.
I knew our family was special.
Mother warned, "Be sure you can always hold your heads up."
Now I wonder if with all Mother's care the
    neighbors may have thought
    we were proud.

Remember Who You Are

Mother had a supply of sayings at the ready,
    like "Remember who you are"
    which she brought out
    when we children went on a trip,
    on a date or to a party.
Mother knew who she was—
    all those generations of
    French and Swiss ancestors before her
    had kept the faith.
I knew I lived in their train,
    but often it felt
    like a burden.
Sometimes I wished I didn't know so well who I was.
Yet at times, to remember helped, setting boundaries as it did.

My children, forgive me and bless me for asking you to
    "Remember who you are."

The Choice

Most farmers in our Illinois community owned their farms,
>   but there were a few rental properties
>   whose tenants moved often.

One March several new children came to school,
>   March being the usual month
>   for farm moves.

Their parents came to the picnic on the last day of school.
>   Two teen-age daughters were with them.
>   Each had a withered arm.

"Polio," Mother whispered. "Don't stare."
>   The family brought a cake with
>   frosting heaped astoundingly high.

Mother would have thought it sinful.
>   Our family's cakes were always frosted too,
>   but in moderation.

Later, moving along the food table,
>   as I neared the chocolate cake
>   my friend Hazel hissed, "Don't take a piece."

I moved on reluctantly, regretfully.
>   If Mother had been nearby
>   she would have made me take a piece.

11/20/97

School Was Important

Mother didn't want us to miss school.
When it was corn picking time
    we needed to help open the field and we did.
But Mother took us to school
    when we were finished so we wouldn't be late.
Only once I remember
    we spent a forenoon picking up potatoes.
When we came in at noon Mother had a special meal for us
    then she took us to school for the afternoon.
Unlike a cousin whose father kept him out of school
    so much that he had to repeat a grade,
    we were in school faithfully in all weather.
We children knew that school was important.
From that rural school we went on to high school
    and college and some to graduate school.

Mother Read to Us

The day the *Farm Journal* came
    Mother read the story in it.
She read at the supper table while we ate.
Did she eat after we had left the table?
Did she imagine how much pleasure it gave us?
Was it part of her plan to raise a family of readers?
I never wondered if other families had stories read to them.
I remember how quietly we ate.
    How good the food tasted!
I remember little of the stories.
I only know that Mother turned out four forever readers.

3/27/99

Our Watkins Man

Our Watkins man stirred up small whirls of dust
    as he drove in our lane.
I only knew him as a summer caller
    He must have also come
    when we children were in school.
Carrying a battered black suitcase
    he knocked on the back door.
    Mother welcomed him into the summer porch.
He returned to the car for a second black suitcase
    then opened them
    showing his goods in neat racks.
There were some things Mother
    bought only from the Watkins man—
    vanilla, cinnamon, a certain kind of ointment.
Sometimes he had a new product and
    Mother considered carefully—
    did we need it? should she buy it?
He did not carry news from the other houses on his route.
    This was not a social call.
    Mother did not offer him coffee.
He left, leaving a faint aroma of spices in the air.
One Sunday, driving home from church,
    we met the Watkins man driving a big fancy car.
    He waved and Mother waved back.
"Why does he have a different car?" I asked.
    "His old car is good for business,"
    Mother said matter-of-factly.
I felt something firm and familiar falling away.
    I wanted the Watkins man out of the shiny, new car,
    back in the little Model A where he belonged.

5/31/97

What Did Mother Fear?

The night gypsies camped along the road south of our house
Was the only time Mother locked the doors.
She knew they would take some of the chickens.
There was a rumor that a horse had been taken in Illinois.
Once Mother said she heard a baby cry in the night.

Mother feared the gypsies.
Was it the mystery that frightened her?
Where did they come from?
Where were they going?
Why did they choose to camp on our lonely road?

By morning they had moved on,
Leaving us to our staid, settled ways.
Perhaps that is what Mother feared,
Being forced to face our rooted lives.

4/25/98

Mother Fed Tramps

We wondered how so many tramps found our farm
    seven miles from the railroad
    and ours a lonely road.
And was it true that they put an "X" at the places
    where the meals were good?
    I could never find an "X."
Mother heaped a plate with food and gave it to him
    on the front porch steps.
    He ate quickly without conversation.
Mother did not hand him a tract, just food.
    Then we watched him shuffle
    down the road.
I had heard that Vachel Lindsey knocked on doors
    and exchanged poems for bread.
    I could see no signs of poetry in our tramps.
They came and went,
    destination unknown,
    perhaps even to them.
Seeing one go, Mother said
    "He was once somebody's little baby."
    It was a thought too sad to think about.

What Did the Preacher Say?

Something this May day quickened a memory.
Mother, her voice bright and light as a girl's
Calling to us, "Come, we will go to the woods
      and see what the little preacher has to say to us."
I could not ever remember Mother leaving work for play
      in such a carefree way.
We careened down the dusty road, every window open,
      our hair flying in the wind.
In the dark quiet woods we found Jack-in-the-pulpit
      standing solemn under his canopy.
Did he know we would never return to the woods?
I thought I heard him say, "Seize the day."
But memory is faint and elusive.
So I do not know what he said.
I do not know.

8/16/97

Lost Stories

I lived in one of those sturdy square houses
    built in the early nineteen hundreds.
They dot the Midwest yet,
    firm as the day they were built.
Where did the cookie cutter pattern come from?
Could it be built from a builder's mail order catalogue?
I know the inside of those houses, too,
    square rooms inside the larger square.
I could find my way in the dark
    in any one of those houses.

Frank Lloyd Wright must have despaired.
He was into Prairie Houses,
    houses that hugged the land,
    that followed its contour.
But farmers would have nothing to do with them.
They wanted a house with a second story and an attic,
    so they could see above the cornfields.
A few even had a widow's walk,
    their men only plowing the back forty.
Even so some never returned home.

There was a porch stretched across the front,
    staring toward a seldom traveled country road.
The porch was a luxury for those whose work was done,
    but the work was never done,
And the stories that might have been told of an evening,
    on that porch, have been lost forever.

4/12/97

Parents

Mother—Mary Graber Conrad Wade Good (1887–1982)
Father—Clark Orrville Detweiler Wade (1891–1934)

Walk Carefully

Walk carefully for
the coming generations
walk in your footsteps.

The Mystery of Ancestors

Their names are etched in stone
    in the little prairie cemetery in Illinois,
      all but Christian, buried in Ohio, dead four years
        after he brought his family to America.
They are traced on my heart, too:
    Verena and Christian Conrad, Esrom and Amelia Wade,
      the grandparents,
    Clark and Mary Conrad Wade, parents.
I arrange them alphabetically,
    then chronologically by birth dates, 1829 to 1891.
I am looking for answers.
I want to know, which one gave me the will to work,
    good health and high energy,
    tensile strength in adversity,
    unshaken faith?
Was there poetry in one, lost in the endless round of work?
Would there still be DNA in the dust of their graves
    to give the answers for which I search?

1/11/03

Mother Was Generous

Mother and Father were generous spirits.
Mother put on special meals for visiting
    ministers and missionaries,
And sent them home with food beside,
    canned fruit and vegetables and jellies.
In season she sent fresh things from the garden.
Father filled their gas tanks from the farm pump,
    and often pressed money into their hands.
Grandmother watching from her rocking chair
    cautioned Father,
        "You should save it for the children."
Grandmother could understand being generous with
    canned goods and jellies,
        for the cellar was full of them.
But money was a different matter.
I think Father understood her concern that
    there might not be enough
        because she had been a widow for twenty-nine years
        and was dependent on her children.
He would still be generous.
Mother and Father loved each other's generous hearts.

Mother Found a Way

Mother needed people.
She would have made a wonderful island woman,
    surrounded by family in the village,
        getting last night's news at the well in the morning.
Instead she was planted on an isolated Illinois farm
    where month followed month of endless work,
    and babies came every two years.
There were the letters from Iowa, but sometimes the
    thread was almost too slender.
Then, before she collapsed physically or mentally,
    she invited her mother and a sister to
    come live with her.
Grandmother had the bedroom and bath on the first floor.
Aunt Lena had the northeast bedroom on the second floor.
Now when Mother's hand was needed in the field,
    or when a migraine struck her down,
    the household work went on,
    the children were lovingly cared for.
The three women lived in the comfort of
    their common heritage.
Sometimes I wondered which one was my mother.
I don't think Mother was ever lonely again.

8/15/98

Mother Was Strong

Father, coming from a family that took church lightly,
Was pleased with Mother's religious devotion.
"If the church door is open, we go," Mother said.
Sunday morning and night, midweek meeting,
    weeks of revival meeting, we went.
Mother seemed energized by the righteous routine.
Where did she learn the pattern?
From home before she went out to work at age twelve?
In one of the houses where she worked for sixteen years?
The mother-in-law was pleased with Mother, too.
Mother said she always kissed her when they met at church.
    (She did not kiss the other daughters-in-law).
At home there were prayers at mealtime and bedtime.
And Mother sang hymns as she worked:
    Rock Of Ages . . .
    Built on a Rock . . .
Now I wonder about those strong hymns.
Was Mother afraid she might not be strong enough?
Was she sometimes weary of being the strong one?

4/25/98

The Topic

Mother was an eternal scholar, although
    her formal schooling was cut off at the age of twelve
    when she began working out.
She worked in the homes of others
    until her marriage at twenty-eight.
Once she took out time to attend a six-week's Bible School.
The little certificate she received gave her
    almost as much confidence as a seminary degree.
With it and the help she received from taking notes,
    from her reading and speakers she heard,
    she was called on regularly to give a topic.
A topic caused her one of the embarrassments of her life.
Standing before the congregation
    she opened her Bible and faced blank papers.
She had mistakenly put her topic on the shelf
    in the basement with her bonnet.
There was nothing to do but go down and retrieve it.
Rising to the occasion the song leader
    led the congregation in a hymn.
Mother returned with two red spots on her cheeks
    and hair slightly disheveled.
She knew her place and stood on the floor
    in front of the pulpit.
Denied its physical and spiritual support,
    Mother delivered her topic,
        not knowing it was really a sermon.

Mother and Norman Vincent Peale

Norman Vincent Peale was very important to Mother.
    She listened to him on the radio.
She read everything that he wrote,
    and she longed to hear him in person.
That dream came true one October Sunday morning
    when she was in New York City visiting a son.
He hailed a taxi, directed the driver to Riverside Church
    where Peale was preaching
    and waved Mother off.
The driver bolted forward as though into rush hour traffic.
    Mother smiled bravely out the window.
At Riverside Church, Mother took notes, carefully.
    She always took notes.
She would share them with her friends in Illinois
    and she would feed on them herself for a long time.
Norman Vincent Peale could not have known that
    in that large audience, his most attentive listener was a
    small woman from the Midwest.
The event was not comparable to
    a Catholic meeting the Pope,
But it came close to it for an elderly Mennonite
    farm woman that morning.

5/1/99

Our Mother the Writer

Sunday afternoon Mother wrote letters,
    except when we had company for dinner.
After the table was cleared she assembled her tools:
    a ruled tablet, sharpened pencil, stamps,
    the packet of letters sent by sisters and brothers,
    friends, cousins, and missionaries.
What did she write?
Certainly about the weather so important to farmers,
    the state of the crops, the family's health,
    the visiting preacher.
There would be nothing of honors we
    children might have received,
    for Mother had been taught well of the sin of pride.
We children knew that Mother's letter writing time was
    as sacred as a devotional hour.
Summers we played outside,
    winters quietly in a corner of the dining room.
Mother had many roles: cook for ten three times a day,
    gardener, church visitor, field hand in emergencies.
But on Sunday she sat
    a high priestess at the dining room table,
    our Mother, the writer.

6/29/97

"Neither Snow Nor Rain Nor Sleet..."

The mailman was an important person to Mother.
She watched for his coming, then ran out to get the mail.
He was Mother's link to the world of relatives and friends
      she had left in Iowa when she moved to Illinois.
When we butchered, Mother put fat links of
      sausage in an empty oatmeal can and
      left it in the mailbox.
We children knew him only as a face in the car window
      to whom we waved when we played in the front yard.
I don't know how Mother learned of his death.
She told us children, her voice flat and dull,
"He took his own life."
Of course the mail still came for
      neither snow nor rain nor sleet
      stopped the courier from his appointed rounds.
But for Mother the mail was edged in black for a long time.

7/11/98

Sunsets

Mother, stirring supper on the stove at the kitchen window,
Watched for the sunsets flung against the sky back of
    the row of walnut trees at the farm's edge.
"Come look!" Mother called to anyone who could hear.

One summer dust and water particles in sunshine struck
    dazzling colors across the sky.
Rembrandt and Degas, with not enough red in their
    paint pots could not have painted those sunsets.
Perhaps Van Gogh and Matisse might have tried.

Mother asked a woman at church,
"Have you seen the wonderful sunsets this summer?"
"No," the woman answered curtly.
    "I don't have time to watch sunsets."
No time to watch sunsets?
"That poor, poor woman," Mother said.

2/27/98

Mother and the Car

After driving horse and buggy
    Mother never quite mastered the car.
Our first car was a 1925 Dodge with snap-on side curtains.
In the winter we huddled under blankets.

Later, Father bought another Dodge with real windows.
"Don't go telling the neighbors," Mother warned.
"They will know we have a new car when we drive past."
Not tell them?
My brother and I ran through the orchard
    to the field across from the neighbors.
We called the good news across the road to them,
    then we crept home.

Mother did not just drive, she careened down the road.
Once, on the way to town, a herd of
    cattle crossed the road in front of her.
Mother thought she had hit a cow but she wasn't sure.
On the way home she saw
    a cow already strung up for butchering.
    Then she knew she had hit it.

The August morning Mother and I were going to town
    to buy school shoes for me,
Father came to the car, leaned on the window smiling.
    "Take care," he said to Mother.
That was the day of the fatal farm accident.
We should have said to Father, "Take care."

When Mother was eighty she was afraid that
she wouldn't pass the driver's test.
Her family was afraid she would.

Perhaps she saw the driver-examiner hesitate.
>   She said to him, "I have to drive.
>   I'm a home visitor for the church
>   and I need to be able to drive to get to my people."
He passed her but said sternly, "Don't drive at night and
>   don't drive out of town."
"Oh, I won't, I won't," Mother said happily.

12/5/98

Mother's Wool Comforters

Mother liked to have sheep on our farm.
They grazed the lower orchard and the upper orchard.
In the spring they were sheared,
    their little lambs waiting for them
    crying under the Wolf River apple tree.
All winter we slept warm and secure, under comforters
    made of their washed and carded wool.
Seventy years later as I sleep
    sheep gambol in my head
    graze the orchards
    sleep in the pale moonlight.
Mother's comforters give more than warmth.

1/27/99

Waiting for Summer

Today the summer sun has painted the flowers gold.
A gentle breeze has played its flute in the pines.
Is this what Mother is waiting for?

Remembering the cruel cold of our father's November burial,
the unforgiving wind at our grandmother's February grave,
Mother had said, "I want to die in the summer."

This bitter December day Mother announces,
"I want to die."
"No, Mother, you cannot die now," we tell her.
"Remember, you want to die in the summer."

Would she remember, so many years later?
Yes, she remembers.
"I will wait for summer," she says.

2/21/04

Our Family Did Not Burn Corn

The year was 1930, depression in the nation,
    in Illinois, on our farm.
With the price of corn so low and
    the price of gas to haul it to the mill so high,
    our neighbors were burning corn for fuel.
My father said, "Corn is food. We will never burn corn."
Come spring the corncribs were still full and the new crop
    was coming on.
Father began hauling corn to a mill in Janesville, Wisconsin.
One of us children went along to keep him company,
    to keep him awake.
I was eleven years old.
We drove past quiet houses, past almost dark towns,
    past fields of sleeping cattle.
What did we talk about?
What songs did we sing?
    I do not know.
    I only know that finally nothing helped.
Father pulled the truck off the road,
    saying he had to sleep awhile.
I walked far down the road.
    When I returned, the sun was cresting the hill.
It outlined the truck listing awkwardly by the road,
    Father sleeping in the cab.
Suddenly I felt a quick rush of pride.
Our family did not burn corn.

2/5/05

Shared Loneliness

I wish I were back in the plain white church
    on the ridge of the Illinois prairie.
(Impossible wish for the church is long since gone,
    replaced by a modern building
    topped with a plastic steeple.)
Father, you would be sitting on the men's side,
    the north side of the church,
    a solitary figure surrounded by many men.
I would be sitting with my mother on the south side,
    with other women and many children,
    in the flat air of Sunday worship,
    where the Spirit longed to descend
    and sometimes did.
I would go to you.
You would take my hand
    and we would walk out together
    into the delicious spring air,
    free from the sermon gone stale on the lips of the
    old minister who must have had a calling once.
We would go home.
We would walk down the pasture lane where a meadowlark
    poised on a fence post would
    sing a deliriously happy tune,
    rescuing us from shared loneliness.

4/22/06

The Brown Suit

Mother went to town with Father to buy him a suit.
It was the first since their wedding day.
At home Father tried it on for us children.
It was a dark brown wool and looked just right
    on our young handsome father.
Then it was hung in the closet waiting for autumn weather.
But one sunny summer day the accident
    crushed our small family.
Our uncle drew Mother weeping away from the coffin.
We children stood nearby, silent, fatherless and afraid,
    so afraid.
It was too fine a suit to wear to the grave.

September 28

This, my father, was your birth-date
For forty-three years.
I remember you.
I remember our life together on the farm.
I remember the day you died—
How all the machinery stopped,
How corn never grew so tall again.

And I learned the way
Childhood can end in a moment and forever.

7/24/96

The Loser at the County Fair

I, a farm girl of long ago, wait on the bleachers
    at the county fair.
At my right is a family with three small boys.
    Does the mother still wish for a girl?
To my left a man with one arm strides up the steps.
I do not doubt that he is still a farmer.
    Farmers don't give up easily.
There are tractors of all sizes, from the big ones
    with air conditioned cabs and stereos
    to the perky little garden tractors.
There are tractors in line for the tractor pull.
I am waiting for the "golden oldies."
A John Deere is hooked to the sled.
    (We were a John Deere family.)
The driver is intense and focused.
He looks like some kind of god controlling his steed.
Suddenly I feel afraid for him.
I remember my father, strong and handsome
    felled that sunny August day in the farm accident,
    the day after my fifteenth birthday. He was forty-three.
The driver is pulling forward but his tractor is losing ground.
He accelerates and terrible black smoke pours out
    and rises like a mushroom cloud.
He knows his machine and knows it can do no more.
Sadness swells in my throat and tears come.
The driver knows now what I feared.
He cannot win.

9/20/03

Dream—June 2005

At a festive gathering of persons,
> not from my present life but from times past,
> I was waiting for my father to arrive.

When he did not come I said,
> "He may have stayed too long in the field."

I was not anxious, knowing he would come.
> Then I saw him at the door.

He was wearing the fine brown wool suit
> he had bought and modeled for us children,
> before hanging it in the closet for autumn wear.

But that was the summer of the accident
> and autumn never came for him.

I walked toward him, so proud of him
> looking young and strong and handsome.

I put my hand on his arm and he drew me to him.
> I felt his warmth.

"Come," I said. "I want you to meet some friends."
Then I awoke and tears came,
> happy tears.

6/18/05

GARDENS

Artist's Delight

Monet would have loved
yellow and black butterflies
circling Queen Anne's lace.

Good Work

You planted a garden east of Eden.
Good work!
I have seen redbud and dogwood lacing the Ozark forest.
I have knelt to see (but not to touch)
    tiny Alpine flowers at the tree line in the Rockies.
I have been warmed by the browns and golds
    of Winterthur in September.
I have walked in wonder under the magnolias
    in Luxembourg Gardens.
Once rounding a curve near Vigan I saw the
    flamboyant tree that would flame in my heart forever.
Now I tend the lilies in my Indiana garden
    and listen to hear Your pleased
"Good work."

The Forager

The travel agent cannot tempt me with his
    tours to exotic places
For I have traveled the earth gathering its treasures:
    asparagus on the Illinois roads of my childhood,
    prickly pear on the stony school-yard in Arkansas
      and persimmon in its woods,
      blackberries and little crab apples along the abandoned
        railroad tracks of Pennsylvania,
    elderberries on Indiana roadsides
    and everywhere the new green of dandelions, and
    puff-balls like manna sprung up overnight.
If the travel agent could offer a tour to such bounty,
I would go at once.

9/8/01

Can We Share a Garden?

The chipmunk under the myrtle
    listens as I weed and water.
Sometimes he peers out (just checking),
    then waits to hear my retreating footsteps.
First he forages under the finch feeder,
    then looks for breakfast crumbs at the picnic table
    before drinking at the little pool
    left by the leaking garden hose.
When I wake in early morning,
    I imagine him drinking dew from the grass,
    nibbling on the violets.
Seeing the late night light at my desk,
    does he wonder if I am writing a poem?
I do not know his name.
He does not know mine,
    but we are not strangers.
Yes, we can share a garden.

11/20/04

The Bouquets

In that sunless room no preacher's voice
    could so illuminate The Word.
Sunday after Sunday she brought
    summer's sweet flowers
Picked so carefully from her garden,
    arranged with such delight.
Her gift to that little drab congregation
    and to God.

10/20/00

Remembering

Today I picked poppies in the garden
    great gorgeous Georgia O'Keefe poppies
        sensuously alive in the noonday sun.
I picked them for you, knowing how they would flame
        on that lonely windswept grave.
But it was too late, so many miles, so many years
        too late.
And already the poppies wilted in my hands
    so I picked the petals off one by one
        and floated them in the garden pool,
            remembering—remembering.

6/1/00

I Need a Letter from Home

Do the August daylilies still define
    the schoolhouse fence in Illinois
    of that long ago happy childhood?
Does the flamboyant tree still bloom with
    surprising beauty on the curve
    of the Vigan road in Luzon?
Do redbud and dogwood still lace
    the Arkansas woods
    with incomparable grace?
Does the gold of coltsfoot on the slag heaps of
    old strip mines in Pennsylvania appear
    where nothing else will ever grow?
I will not see these again.
I only carry them in memory's trace.
Yet I need a letter from home.
Write and tell me that they still live
    and bless hungry hearts.

5/20/06

Simone Barbadillo's Garden

Simone Barbadillo's garden on the edge of Bangued, Abra
    in the Philippines
    was a small green paradise.
There we sat in the shade of a mango tree
    while Simone served us papaya and rice in braided
    banana leaves and a pineapple drink in
    small coconut bowls.
Mornings, on the way to market, he brought us flowers,
    frangipani, bougainvillea, and orchids.
Lying awake in the stifling heat of night
    I thought of Simone's garden
    and tried to forget the shadow hovering over it.
For every year as the hot dry season lingered,
    Simone became distraught and ran naked into town.
The police put him in jail,
    where he stared out the barred window,
    his wild eyes searching the sky for rain.
When the rain came he grew calm and could go home.
Simone was friend and kin to me.
For though I had no garden to tend,
    my parched soul thirsted for rain.

7/14/01

A Bitter End

The year a robin built her nest in the little basket
    on the ledge at the kitchen door,
        we felt honored.
We used the front door often so we would not disturb
    the robin at her nest.
Then just before the little birds were old enough to fly,
    tragedy struck.
One morning we found the baby robins
    torn in bloody pieces
    scattered on the deck floor,
    prey of a night hungry raccoon.
For several days their mother wandered on the lawn bereft,
    then finally left.
I told our naturalist friend
    we would take the basket down,
    that never again would a robin build in it.
"No," he said, "what happened is the way of life;
    one must accept it.
The robin will build again to raise her family
    or to have it destroyed.
Take your place in the rhythm of life
    and do not be bitter."
I was not bitter, but I was very sad.
Now, remembering, I am still sad.

2/15/03

Our Summer Pheasant

I remember the summer day I first saw the pheasant
    hopping on the garden path,
    hopping as any creature hops with only one leg.
Trailing his long tail like a train,
    he hopped between the rows of radishes and peas,
    beans and beets, cabbage and carrots.
He never spoke or sounded a note.
He was a spot of color in our green world.
I liked to think he felt safe in our garden.
He must have known we were not hunters.
With October he was gone.
Did the hunter know this pheasant had only one leg?
    Did he care?

I miss his silent presence in the garden.
I miss the sun glinting on his autumnal colors.
I miss his modeling courage in a wounded world.

8/30/03

Calendar Garden

We walk in the Calendar Garden at DeFries Park
    as night closes in.
The woods at its edge loom black,
    not menacing but protecting.
The lilies in the pool have folded their pink petals.
A still-awake bullfrog gives a solemn croak.
Nearby somewhere a bird is crooning
    a very soft sound.

We watch the yellow and white flowers
    turn quickly gray.
We pick a few late wild strawberries,
    savoring their goodness,
    the last of summer's sweetness.
The sky is starless
    as we walk from the garden.
    Small raindrops fall on us.
How blessed I am to have captured
    this October garden in memory,
    and to have been a lifelong member
    of God's wonderful world.

11/17/07

Winter's Way

White is winter's way
      with birch branches
      white on white,
      weeping willows
      brave in white,
      last summer's nest
      filled with white,
      last summer's green
      numb with white.
White is winter's way.

Remembered

Memory

Treat it carefully.
Memory wields an adz that
can sharpen sadness.

The Two-Cent Copper Coin

I awoke.
I lay in the heavy darkness for a long time
    reciting the losses of my life:
A beloved house and its yard and garden,
    my watch, an engagement present,
    a dear, I thought forever, friendship.
Losses failed to induce sleep.
"Try remembering things you found," I told myself.
At once the very first thing I found came to mind.
In the sunny August garden my eight-year-old bare foot
    turned up a two-cent coin.
It must have lain there a long time,
    for it was a coin unfamiliar to me.
It lay near the small white peach tree
    in the garden fencerow.
The tree did not bear heavy fruit, like the trees
    in the upper and lower orchards.
That day the ripening peaches sweetly scented the air.
Bees circled the fruit that had fallen to the ground.
I started to run to show Mother,
    but before I reached the house,
I slept.

5/4/02

The Schoolhouse Walk

A learned man in prison observed that we are all exiles
    if only from childhood.
I remember fleeing childhood
    lusting for imagined freedom.
I remember slamming the door behind me,
    thinking I would never return.
Now an eternity later
    I journey to my birthplace.
I walk again the dusty country road to school.
This September day goldenrod and asters line the roadside
    just as I remember.
Sulphur butterflies hover over rotting fruit
    under the row of hedge apple trees.
A beetle solemnly pushes his dung ball ahead of him,
    how many generations after the first beetle
    I saw on that road?
It was only when the meadow lark on a fence post
    sang his joyous song—five ascending and
    two descending notes—over and over
    that I felt the lightness of a
    long forgotten freedom.
Now on the road toward exile,
    I knew I could walk that dusty road
    forever.

9/19/98

Miss Coney

Third year English at Sterling High School
      was a required course taught by Miss Coney.
She was small and had wrinkles.
I thought she was very old.
      (Perhaps she was not really that old.)
I remember the room.
It seemed airy and light.
      (With only a few windows, was it really that light?)
It seemed like a haven
      after the agony of algebra,
      the tedium of Latin conjugations.
Entering from the narrow dark hall
      crowded with noisy students
      was like being washed ashore
      to a safe harbor where the pilot
      had a passion for Blake and Dickinson.
I remember Miss Coney with joy.

5/21/05

Rayma Rawson

Rayma Rawson from Strawberry Point, Iowa
    taught English at Sterling High School.
She combed her dark hair almost over one eye.
She wore red, red lipstick and a ring watch.
    I could have swooned when she gracefully
    flung her hand into the air to check the time.
The school board had hired a teacher too
    exotic for our small town
    so her tenure would be short.
But that woman knew book starvation when she saw it.
She knew that living in the country seven miles from town
I was denied a public library card, even though
    in bold letters over the door it read
    "Free to all!"
One day as I left the classroom, Miss Rawson held
    her library card out to me.
"I want you to have it this year," she said.
Stunned, I spoke a small "thank you."
Some day I would wear make-up
    and I would own a ring watch, too,
    but not yet, not yet.
For now I would read that library dry.

Memory

I count them memory by memory
    grateful they have not hit the cutting room floor.
I count them like beads on a rosary
    until I come to the painful one,
    the old, old one,
    the unforgiving one.
I ask my Guide, "Must I keep this one forever?"
"Forever," he answers firmly.
"Even that memory is proof that you lived.
Remember nothing really happened unless it is remembered."

I know one cannot program memory,
    but I would like to save today:
    the sweetness of lilacs in the sun,
    the incredible joy of the wren in the redbud,
    the glorious sense of well-being.
I wonder, could I replace the hurtful memory
    with this joyful one?
I wonder, would I be able to explain it to my Guide?

4/26/03

The Flamboyant Tree

That August morning we left Bangued, Abra,
Where only three houses remained
In the Philippine town of 7,000 after the war.
The trees had gone with the houses. The birds were gone too.
I mourned their irreparable loss.

When we rounded the curve in the road to Vigan
The flamboyant tree burst on our sight
Like fireworks on the 4th of July.

Flung against the bluest of skies
Were flowers the size of roses
In shades of almost crimson to almost orange.
The showiest tree in the world intoxicated my lagging spirits.
I turned to watch the tree as long as it was in sight.

Now, half a world away and fifty years later,
I wonder if the flamboyant tree still blooms
At the curve in the Vigan road.

There is no one to tell me.
I tell myself I do not need to know,
For it blooms in my heart forever.

5/1/02

Going Home

It is not hard to say good-bye for we are going home.
I dream that we will return one day
>to see the rubble of war cleared away
>to find the rice fields green and productive
>perhaps to eat fruit from the trees we planted.

We have been thanked for our service at farewell programs.
On this last morning in the half dark, Felo, our faithful cook
>prepares a large breakfast,
>for he traveled to Manila once and knows
>the hard bridgeless road ahead of us.

As promised the bus arrives at dawn,
>grinding its gears and pouring out black smoke.

Our baggage is loaded, all the gifts for the family in America,
>all the fruit from the tropics—a coconut, many swa.

We take no eggs but I think of the gift egg
>that hatched out on the kitchen table.

Then I see them standing at the gate,
>four women from a distant village.

One holds out a little knotted gray cloth to me.
I untie it and see ancestral beads,
>the beads passed down from mothers to daughters.

There are the yellow beads traded with China 500 years ago,
>the small brown beads
>whose history no-one remembers
>two agates each worth a carabao
>if the family's beast of burden should die.

"Naimbag a begat," I say in the Ilocano I have never mastered.
I do not lift my eyes from the soft dirt of our street,
>no longer our street.

We are going home.
Then why this sudden stab of loss, as final as a last farewell?

12/14/96

Quaker Meeting

Past the tall spires shouting "church"
    past the bell towers blaring "church music"
    to the little white meetinghouse.
The room is lit by the soft light
    of clear windows looking into winter trees.
I wait and wait and wait,
    willing someone to speak.
George Fox, Lucretia Mott, Rufus Jones,
    was it so hard your first time
    before the holy quiet stilled your restless hearts?
I need a word from you, Lord.
"If Thou wouldst have me be a Friend,
    Thou must center me down."

3/4/04

The Happy Hour

I remember reading to the children
    sitting on the lumpy couch
    in our third floor apartment at the mission school
    in the Ozark National Forest.
We sat squeezed together, the better to see the pictures.
No one complained "She touched me" or "I can't see."
It was the fairy book moment of love and accord—
    the home beautiful.
I did not skip one page or miss one word for
    these little worn books had been memorized.
Eyes widened in fear for Madeline when
    Miss Clavel turned on the light and cried
    "Something is not right."
They sighed in relief when Peter Rabbit,
    given up for lost,
    was saved at last from Mr. McGregor.
They caught their breath when the four
    burly policemen at the corner of Beacon Street
    held back the traffic so Mrs. Mallard and her ducklings
    could safely march across the street.
The smallest cried when the shepherd
    found his little black lamb
    and carried him safely in his arms down the mountain.
"Perhaps we should not read this one," I suggested gently.
    "No, read," she insisted, "It is not bad to cry."
The shades were drawn, holding the dark at bay.
The door was locked against the sorrows that lurked.
Our little family was safe inside.

3/3/01

The Bird Nest

It was evening and time for our guests to arrive.
The toys were picked up
The table was set
The children were bathed
The meal was almost ready.
The guests were coming from Mother's town.
I wanted them to report how well they found us.
(Do daughters want to please their mothers
    as long as they live?)
"Go outside," I urged the children
"See who can be the first to hear the car coming."
It would be the only car coming on our lonely road.
They left. Then I heard them return
And go into the bathroom.
Soon they called, "Come, we have a surprise."
There on the flush box sat a large tin can
Crowned by a round muddy lump.
Red Arkansas clay dripped down the side of the can,
Down the side of the flush box,
Down onto the floor.
The children had clay on their hands
And down their fronts.
"It's a nest," they said.
Their eyes fixed eagerly on me.
I knew well that only a bird or a child could
    make the miracle of a nest.
I stood struck speechless,
Knowing I was about to fail a test.

6/9/01

The Night Blooming Cereus

Our neighbor, Mrs. Lynn, called,
"Our Cereus is going to bloom tonight. Can you come?"
This was the flower that bloomed one night a year.
At dusk we walked to the Lynn's.
We saw the plant against the house,
    its tight cream-colored buds waiting to open.
We sat in a semi-circle and waited, too.
Other neighbors gathered but we did not talk.
The children sat in the grass, eyes intent on the Cereus.
It was like church,
    church without hymns or a sermon,
    just a kind of holy quiet.
At dark we saw the flowers slowly open
    looking like magic roses.
Then Mrs. Lynn served cake and coffee
    and we turned to conversation.
How did the Cereus know to bloom on this one night?
Could Mrs. Lynn know she would give us a lifetime memory?

12/7/02

The Gift

My child, my little child and I
Stand at the window and see the leaves of the trees
    lit like a thousand lamps in the evening sun.
"If little girls could pick some leaves they would
    give them to their mothers," she said, and hesitated.
"I will get you a gift," she said.
I watched her go to the sweet gum tree.
I saw how small she seemed under the tall tree.
I watched her jump and reach for leaves, not able to choose,
    just reaching for some.
"Please," I begged, "let some be low enough for her to reach."
Then she came back running,
    her short three-year-old legs going fast.
When she saw me at the window,
    she held up a handful of leaves.
I hurried to meet her at the door.
"I brought you leaves," she said. "Some are red, and
    some are green, and some are yellow."
She coughed importantly.
It had been a long journey.
"They are beautiful," I said.
Then I kissed her little pink cheeks and blew on her neck
    to make her laugh,
    and to cover the lump of love in my throat.
My child, my little child, can not know that
    she herself was the gift.

1/6/00

Carver School—Room 37

At Carver Junior High School
    Chloe was giving her social studies report,
    that is, she was trying to give it.
To distract her, the room was humming.
She fumbled. Color rose in her dark cheeks.
Suddenly, I was very angry at the injustice.
Just because of their collective boredom,
    the class had no right to be cruel.
I pounded my fist on the desk
    and shouted, "Shut Up!"
"Oh, Mrs. Alderfer", a girl in the front row said quietly,
    "You don't say that."
(It was not allowed in my childhood home,
    not anywhere, and not here.)
I apologized to the class.
The room went silent, a dead unprotective silence.
Chloe continued in a soft, shaky voice.
I looked into the sea of sullen faces.
My dream on becoming a teacher
    had been to teach so well that
    every eye would light up.
That dream lay shattered on the Carver School floor.

1/10/04

On the Birth of Granddaughter Greta

Hello, little girl,
Wailing your first good-bye,
Not knowing that hellos and good-byes
Ride tandem through life.
Cease your crying, little new one.
Birth day is also hello time.

6/12/83

Rejoice and Be Glad
For Elaine and Harold,
on their marriage in later life

Love, as mysterious as the sweep of the sky
    with its eternal stars,
        comes.
Comes knowing no time—morning, noon or evening.

God, like a loving mother, like a strong father, says
    "Take this bread and wine,
    communion for your hungry hearts."

God, who makes all things lovely pronounces,
    "This is good."

We ring a peal of bright bells.
We sing sunny songs of joy,
    on this nuptial day.
Rejoice and be glad.

7/15/06

Two Greyhounds in New York City

Walking on Riverside Drive twenty-five years ago
    one sunny autumn morning,
I met a woman with two greyhounds on a leash.
The dogs walked in synchronized rhythm with a royal air.
Did they know they are of an ancient breed,
    their pictures on Pharaoh's tomb in Egypt in 4000 BC?
    Perhaps Moses had greyhounds as his pets.
The woman wore a gray dress that matched the dogs' coats.
By the flare of the skirt and the soft lines,
    I thought "silk".
They could have been a living portrait
    stepped from MOMA on West 53rd Street.
Did she always wear a gray silk dress to match their coats?
I never met them again,
yet the visual pleasure of that glimpse
has never faded.

3/25/07

The Trains of My Life

1928: Awake in the farmhouse bedroom
    of my childhood home
    I heard the lonesome whistle of the train
    seven miles away bound for Chicago.

1937: How many trains traveled on the tracks
    at the edge of Goshen College
    their whistles boldly punctuating every campus event?

1942: I saw a train carrying war machinery
    wending its way across a country gone to war
    and in that moment war came true for me.

1947: At a train station I cried goodbye to the one I loved
    going 13,000 miles away,
    not knowing for how long.

2005: Today I saw 150 mobile houses
    traveling south by train to New Orleans,
    carrying hope for the Katrina homeless.

2006: In sleepless nights I hear the mournful whistle
    and remember Thomas Wolfe writing
    that if there would be a national sound
    it should be the train whistle.

6/17/06

Counted Treasures Remain

Today I count my treasures,
golden as the day they were minted:

kittens born under the lacy
bower of the asparagus.
the plaintive cry of the mourning dove
just before the rain clouds broke.

fireflies rising from the grass,
driving back the waiting dark.
the wondrous amazing scent
of noontime new mown hay.
honeysuckle, their tiny drops of nectar
sweetest, sweetest honey on the tongue.

I hold in memory's trace:
the pine grove at the farm's edge.
the soughing of the wind.
the crisp crunch of needles underfoot,
sun-patterned and warm.
the plaintive voice of the mourning dove.

Ah, time you have taken much,
but these you have not touched.

4/89

The Particulars of My Life

This is the particular landscape of home.
I know it well.
I know how sunrises tip the tops of the maples,
    then travel quickly down branch by branch.
I know how sunsets light the maples
    like burning bushes.
I listen to the wren guarding the nest
    in the gourd swinging on the redbud tree.
I wait for the chipmunk in the stone wall,
    who waits for breakfast crumbs.
I trace the geese calling south,
    then north.
I watch the fireflies, small points of hope,
    rise in the gathering dark.
I see night creep gently across the grass,
    stilling the songs of birds.
God comes very close to me in the particulars.

8/31/02

Reflections

Winter Trees

So, this is the shape
of the leafless trees, winsome
in simplicity.

Waiting for a Poem

"Wait in silence for a poem to come,"
the poetry teacher advised.
I wait and wait.
How long did you wait, Robert Frost, for
    "Two roads diverged in a yellow wood. . ."
How long, Sandburg, for "The fog came on little cat feet."
And, David, how long for "The Lord is my Shepherd,
    I shall not want."
A cardinal in the hawthorn calls over and over,
    seven notes, a pause, then six more notes.
He has found his poem.
A bee circles the honeysuckle three times,
    then lights to gather nectar.
She has found her poem.
I wait, but now the waiting is not so hard.

8/24/99

Hymn to the Sun

I salute the sun, sign of God's love,
    millions of years old
and stocked with enough fuel to heat the world
    billions of years more.
Oh, magnanimous sign of God's love.

9/9/00

He Finds His Poem

Negro Mountain was ablaze with October's finest
        as I sped on Route 40 toward Grantsville, Maryland
        for an afternoon of poetry at Yoder School.
There I passed a basket of small shells
        gathered at the Atlantic Ocean,
        so foreign, so far away from Yoder School.
"Choose one," I instructed the children,
        "then describe your shell."
A little Amish boy chose a black shell with ridges.
I saw him carefully count the ridges then write
        "My shell has seven furrows
        plowed by miniature horses and miniature men."
The distant ocean
        and the familiar fields
        come together in one small boy's head
        and he finds his poem.

2/11/06

Liberation

How many doilies had she crocheted?
Neat little, tight little circles,
    washed and starched
    she gave them as gifts
    and people thanked her politely.
One windy March day, about to begin
    yet one more doily,
    she saw a small boy cross the lawn.
He knocked on the door and asked,
    "Would you have string for my kite?"
Never having been asked for string before,
    she hesitated, but being quite old and wise
    gave her ball of thread to the boy.
It seemed such a liberating thing to do,
    to give the thread that would lift the
    kite high into the blue,
    to save the thread from a small, tight,
    neat little prison.

The Little Grapes

I pick the small sweet grapes
    ripened by September suns.
I wonder, were they planted
    by the first woman on this land,
    lonesome for her childhood home?
"We will plant grapes
    from the roots of Mother's old vines," she said.
Did she hope they would lighten
    the homesick in her heart?
Remembering the long gone woman,
    today we commune together,
    eating the small sweet fragrant grapes.

10/9/02

October 28

The Artist painted our town with incredible reds and golds.
But when the rains came they turned softer and more muted,
    the way Monet would have painted them
    in his later years of failing eyesight.
October 28 we found a walnut on the doorstep
    winter's calling card signed by a squirrel.
So it was no surprise when the geese flew over that night,
    just hours ahead of cold and snow.
They flew in long wavering V's, calling urgently to each other.
The very old startled awake, then lay back wearily
    remembering other nights and slept.
The little sick child woke crying,
    asking for yet one more drink.
The lovers smiled wordlessly, then turned to each other
    in the dark in total bliss.
Only the poet no longer slept,
    searching for the message hidden in their cries
    long after the geese were out of sound.
Failing to find words for it,
    he turned his face to the wall and wept.

1/11/97

The Happy Family
As told to me by a friend

Christmas Eve our father took us to Allentown
    to see the lights. He drove slowly and silently
    up and down the streets.
Mother sat in the front seat holding Jimmy, with the
    twisted mouth that would never speak and the
    twisted legs that would never walk.
We sisters sat in the back leaning forward,
    eager, anxious not to miss one glorious light.
We hugged ourselves with joy.
    We cried, "Look, look, look" at the
    dazzling trees, the twinkling bushes.
Here in the close dark car we were safe.
    No one could turn away or stare.
    No one could ask, "What is wrong with the boy?"
This was the best of Christmas.
    Oh, Holy blessed night.
In the warm dark car we were like other families.
    We were a happy family.
    But why was our mother crying?

He Cried, Too
A Friend's Story

At the service,
at the grave
they whispered, "She is doing so well."
A few tears, a few sad words,
    but tensile strength holding her
    straight and near calm.

Within six months she married,
    tired of lonely nights,
    of having no one to care,
    no one to share.

One day she knew she had not grieved enough.
Tears came and she walked blindly
    across the dry autumn grass
    to the little garden house.
    There she cried and cried.

Her new husband came to her
and sat beside her without a word
    and cried with her.
Their worlds came together.

10/8/05

Keys

Keys are so small, so easily lost.

How many keys were lost in the Titanic,
Keys that locked a thousand state rooms
Yet could not stay the water that rushed in.

How many keys were lost in the rubble of the towers,
Useless and rusting now in a New Jersey landfill
Never, never to be recovered.

I had five keys to five houses,
All lost now, the houses and the keys,
Real only in fleeting dreams.

I was given keys to knowledge,
Science, religion and philosophy.
Some were successful, some failed.

I had a key designed to open hearts.
It would not fit a lock until the day
It sweetly turned and furnished bread and roses for life.

There yet remains one key,
The key promising eternal life.
I guard it well.

11/17/01

Moving

All those moving vans moving
    east to west, west to east,
    south to north, north to south.
These are not '49 Goldrushers,
    not immigrants crossing borders,
    not refugees looking for a home.
This is America eternally moving,
    sheep driven by a dream of greener pastures.

We follow our van traveling hundreds of miles
    in our seventh move in fourteen years.
We have carefully packed and duly insured
    Grandmother Conrad's dowry chest from France,
    Great Grandfather Detweiler's
    cherry rope bed from Lancaster,
    the deacon's bench from Buck's County,
    along with the accumulation of life,
    furniture, books, dishes, children's toys. . .
Only the cherished memories we do not entrust to the van.
    Fragile yet durable they travel in our heads
    and ride with us in the car.
Pray that they arrive safely.

11/18/06

Waiting for Tomorrow in Assisted Living

When a flight of stairs looks as daunting as Mt. Kilimanjaro
Where gourmet meals taste like sawdust
    to those who have no appetite
When energy is so low that it is impossible
    to imagine that one once ran fleet of foot
    in the meadows of childhood
Where table conversation concentrates on
    pain, sleepless nights and pills,
    not blood pressure-raising religion and politics
When those with arthritic joints can predict a storm
    hundreds of miles away
Where old familiar clothes have become
    either too small or too large
Where a dead mailbox can hurt all day.

Do not be deluded.

These are passengers in a boat in a safe harbor
    with pilots of skill and compassion,
    ready to hear the fears and doubts that come
    when night closes in.

1/20/07

Who Will Sing the Songs?

The Iraqi poet Mikhail mourned,
    "The sky has lost all of its stars."
The exiles, the displaced, the refugees
    wait in starless nights.
Those who sleep on park benches in summer,
    on grates in the sidewalk in winter, wait.
Those who ride the buses all night, wait.
Those captive in nursing homes, waiting, waiting,
    longing to go Home, wait.
The Israelites cried,
    "Here in a foreign land
    how can we sing about the Lord?"
Who can sing a song for the homeless,
    strangers in alien lands?
Yes, who will sing for the homeless?

5/31/03

Transformation Mennonites USA

Even the hopeful-sounding title of transformation
    carries change on its unwieldy back—
    change that, good or bad,
    wrenches us from the familiar,
    the cherished comfortableness,
    and always comes with a price.
Those who do not jump ship
    have something every day to pity and forgive.
What will history write of this disparate people
    who lived through centuries of change,
    sometimes displaced and sometimes martyred?
That we became a people known for unity
    despite the differences that tugged
    and sometimes tore us apart?
That we forged new patterns of justice and peace?
That we lived with amazing grace?

12/10/05

Questions

Preparing for my winter years,
    I have questions:
Thomas Merton, happy in your hermitage,
    "How did you come to a union
    of deep solitude and great concern for the world?"
Dag Hammarskjold, writing in your white book,
    "How did your life relate to what your pen wrote,
When you wrote
    'For what has been—thanks!
    For what is to come—yes'?"
And my Lord, creating the prayer for your disciples,
    "Did you know how hard 'Not my will but thine'
    would be for your disciples,
    would be for this disciple?"

4/9/05

Portent

September, with waves of goldenrod in the meadow and
    the sweetness of grapes on the sunny air,
    seemed eternal.
Perhaps the pattern of the centuries would be broken,
    and there would be no winter.
But someone small was not deluded.
One day a nest appeared in the bookshelf on the wall
    of the meditation house in the garden.
Nestled between Baille's *A Diary of Prayer*
    and Merton's *The Seven Story Mountain*,
    fashioned of pages 1 -78 of *I Francis* by Carretto.
Almost white, it had only a hint of print.
Not being a theologian how did the little mouse know
    that truth, even though shredded,
    could temper the terrors of winter?

Husband
Edwin Stover Alderfer (1922–2004)

August 12, 1944

That brave August day
we bonded our hearts to love
to eternity.

The Wedding Day
August 12, 1944

On this sunny August day chicory and Queen Anne's lace
    grace the Illinois roadside.
Red winged blackbirds call o-ka-leee
    in a ripening field of grain.
I ride to the little white church,
    the church of my parents and grandparents.
On this golden day I am about to marry my heart's desire.
We stand before the people, not touching, like strangers.
The old minister in his rusty black plain suit
    delivers a weary message often given before.
"Hurry, hurry," I want to say.
"We want to begin living happily ever after."
Then come the admonishments to care for each other
    in sickness and in health.
We have no imagination for sickness, never having been ill.
My almost husband has spent the summer
    following the wheat harvest from Texas to Colorado.
    He is tanned and fit.
We answer "I will" glibly and innocently.
    We cannot know the great joys and great sorrows
    that await us.
Finally we sit down to the wedding dinner.
I announce that I am very hungry.
A wedding guest says primly,
    "You are not supposed to be hungry."
But I am hungry, hungry for the lovely dinner,
    for our wedding night, for our life together.
My new husband and I hold hands under the table
    covered with the chaste white linen tablecloth.

10/2/02

August 12, 1944

You mounted a diamond
>in memory's trace
>that August day—
>There when life was greening,
>its dreams inexplicable,
>its measurements all inexact.

Only time would prove
>how priceless the beginning
>of that high hour.

Our Anniversaries

For years we celebrated our August 12th anniversary
    every month, then went traditional and
    honored the day once a year.
You gave me candy and special fragrances,
    once a household tool—
    then apologized for its usefulness.
I baked your favorite foods,
    (even tried to duplicate your mother's cheesecake,
    but never succeeded.)
Once I gave you a trip around the world,
    to be taken when there was money.
    (Of course there was never money,
    but I had the joy of giving you an extravagant dream.)
Forgive me.
I could not celebrate this year.
We never drew a blueprint for celebrating alone.

9/11/04

2003

Night comes slowly,
    darkness falling gently through the great maples,
    dimming the flowers in the garden,
    shadowing the windows of the house.
It is a house that knows only illness.
The pills, the exercises, nourishing food—
    the faithful rituals are still followed.
They have almost forgotten that other life.
They welcome the coming night
    with its promise of grateful sleep.
They sit together a while in the darkness,
    waiting to hear the click,
    as night closes the garden gate to day.

2/17/06

The Journey

Edwin Stover Alderfer (March 12, 1922)

Get on board, little boy.
I have been expecting you.
Take your place.
There will be passengers getting on at every stop.
Choose your seatmates carefully.
You will see fields of golden flowers,
    and the luring lights of big cities.
You will be tempted to get off.
Do not yield to temptation.
Expect frightening black tunnels.
(Some refer to them as the dark night of the soul.)
You will come to fertile fields. Rejoice!
You will come to barren fields. Do not despair.
The train will go on.
There will be unexpected delays,
    perhaps even derailments.
Remember the journey is as important as the inn.
I will be with you to the end of the line.
Your ticket will tell you when to disembark.

Edwin Stover Alderfer (May 21, 2004)

5/21/04

The Killdeer

When my brother and I went to the pasture
    to fetch the cows for milking,
    a killdeer rose out of the grass,
    feigning a broken wing to lure us away from her nest.

Now my husband is dead,
    our children have flown.
    I am alone in the house.
    I have nothing to protect.

Yet when night closes in,
    casting long shadows where sun had lately lain,
    I feel a kinship to the killdeer,
    knowing I did not fully understand her terror.

7/31/04

The Sorrows

If you will tell me your sorrows,
    I will tell you mine.

Tell you how the flowers lost their colors,
    and like ghosts stared into the sun,
  how the birds still sang
    in voices that had lost their tunes.

Remember, I told myself:
  the sun still rises,
    still sets.

Remember how you shared the kiss of rain
    on the eager leaves after drought,
  how you rode into the double rainbow
    on that Colorado road,
  how the wild geese in the abysmal dark
    heading home, called us to love.

Now I am ready—tell me your sorrows.

8/14/04

Tears

Singing the poignant hymn
    "And I will raise you up at the last day,"
Catching a glimpse of dew on a perfect rose,
    (You would have loved to capture it with your camera)
Hearing the plaintive cry of the whip-poor-will near night,
These call for tears.

Meeting a friend, also on a solo journey,
    We talk of other times and other places.
She confides, "I don't cry in public.
    I don't want to make people sad.
    I wait to cry until I get home."

"I know," I tell her,
"But temporal though the earth is, it also is our home.
    It's all right to cry at home."

8/2/05

The Giving Away

It is time to move on,
    time to begin the giving away.
First the books, a lifetime collection:
    theology, psychology, nature,
    flowers, trees, birds,
    the shelf of books on humor.
    (He did so want to have a light heart.)
Next the files: counseling records, talks given,
    business accounts, correspondence, saved articles.
Then the clothes: the well-worn tan corduroy jacket,
    the colorful tie collection,
    last the cherished hat from England.
I box the bee equipment, the candy-making tools and recipes.
Only the fifty-pound marble slab sunk into the countertop,
    especially for making his famous peanut brittle,
    will remain.
Finally the car, rich in memories of rides
    in the greening springtime, the fleeting autumn.
The house is empty now. I lock the door.
No it was not easy.
    But harder is what Emily Dickinson describes as
    the sweeping up of the heart
    and putting love away until eternity.

12/16/06

Our Gardens

I would like to walk with you
    in the gardens we planted,
    walking slowly, slowly
    with shared delight
    in the lush red peonies,
    the sensuous pink poppies,
    the shy sweet lily-of-the-valley,
    the surprising daylilies with their beauty for a day,
    the luxurious Van Gogh sunflowers.
Slowly, slowly walking toward night and sleep.
I'm so glad we were alive together in this world.

8/26/06

Resurrection

In the quiet waiting dark
I count the gold you have poured
   into the coffer of my life:
     a springtime meadow awash with golden flowers,
     a delight of goldfinch undulating
     in the summer sun,
     the liquid gold of the wren's glad song,
     a lifetime of sunrises to dazzle the eyes,
     a million maple leaves dancing to the ground,
     the thin gold circle of our bonding ring.
These have rolled the stone away from my heart.

10/9/04

MORTALITY

Mortality

Ah, mortality
I saw the shadow of your dark wings
brush the sun today.

Instructions to Adam and Eve

Don't try the garden gate latch
    or think of climbing over the fence.
Eden is closed to you forever.
You will want to put down roots now.
    Don't put them down too deep,
    for I have travel plans for you.
Don't dream of being tourists on a tour bus
    with matching polyester suits and Samsonite luggage.
And don't think you can capture the Grand Canyon
    or Niagara Falls with your Nikon.
Be alert to life where you are,
    the total white of winter,
    the surprising greens of spring.
You will want to build a house.
Don't over-furnish it and fill it with stuff.
They are dust, even as you will become.
You will have children
    wanting to play soccer and take music lessons,
    greatly complicating your lives.
Above all, tend well your inner garden.
That is where the true riches are.
I will give you a map.
Bon voyage.

4/17/04

They Also Lived

There are two fields that will never yield a harvest.
At Normandy stone crosses, row on row,
Are washed by summer rain today.
But there will never be enough rain to grow a crop
    in this barren field.
In Washington, 490 feet of ground was plowed
    to bear the granite slabs etched with 50,000 names.
Maya Lin, who designed the Vietnam Wall, said
    "It will make you cry."
But not all the tears shed there will bear fruit.
This was a one time sowing of bitter loss.
Each name holds a history of death,
    whose grief can only be borne by remembering
    that it is also a sign that someone lived.

2/3/01

Missing in Action

Because he is too small to understand
    he silently sits and waits
      in a house stopped by sorrow.
When he can speak, he asks,
    "Will our daffodils bloom?"

1/91

Which Shade of Black?

At Yoder's Department Store I shop
    for material for a quilt.
I am looking for black.
I find fourteen shades of black.
Amazing!
I knew there were a multitude of tints of blue,
    borrowed from the sky,
        a myriad shades of red from sunset's palette,
    uncounted hues of yellow in summer's flowers.
But fourteen shades of black?

Today I woke to clouds heavy with rain,
    frightening stories on national news,
    word of a friend's serious illness.
Which shade of black would fit today?

12/13/03

Emily's Secret

No one knocked at 208 North Main Street, Amherst.
It was not a door that opened easily.
Emily Dickinson wrote, "The Soul selects her own society
    Then shuts the door."
Even in fantasy I cannot knock on that door.
Sometimes reading the poems, I feel I have
    invaded her privacy.
She lived in the house her grandfather built,
    leaving it only once after her father died.
Cloistered in that house she wrote 1,700 poems,
    many of them on the theme of death.
Did writing of death make her morbid?
Once she wrote, "I told my heart to be happy."
Was happiness in the sunset at the westward window,
In the turning of the seasons at the eastward window?
Did she note the tender green of spring,
    the dazzling colors of autumn?
Did her heart quicken to hear the cry of the loon at night,
    the first bird songs at dawn?
She does not tell us.
Was happiness in the acceptance of death,
    completed on that final day
    riding in the carriage away from Amherst,
    when she "first surmised the horse's heads
    were toward eternity?"
I wish I knew.

The Leavetaking

The September day she left there were tomatoes
    ripening on the sill,
       pears at the back door waiting to be canned,
       a quilt in the frame.
Always when a call came
    to a birthing or a dying she took her apron off,
    hung it on the hook, closed the door,
    and went.
This call seemed much like the others,
    and yet, somehow different.
She would have liked to have left things neater.
But those who would fault her
    for this last leavetaking
      must know they do not understand
      the rhythms of her life.

2/22/97

Summer Cannot Be Stayed

The leaves must have fallen from the trees in Indiana
    for all the leaves have fallen in Central Park.
Nine floors down the Hudson is cold and gray,
    emptied of summer boats and summer birds.
The flower vendors on the street
    have put on their little woolen caps.
Our doctor comes in; he is young and strong
    and very kind.
He studies the chart carefully, then says,
    "I see signs of stability."
But there is no hope in his voice,
    for he, too, knows that summer cannot be stayed.

Gathered Home

They shared a table on the Illinois farm—
Mother, Father, Grandmother, Aunt Lena, brother Ralph.
Now they share a small space in the cemetery
    beside the church.
The table grace,
    "Be present at our table, Lord
      And grant that we may feast with Thee in paradise"
    has been fulfilled.
        Amen.

Senescence*

The luminous light
    moments before dark
Has fired the maple
    like Moses' God-lit bush.

Not the gentle light
    of morning,
Not the garish light
    of noon-day,
could so illuminate.

This tree was born
    for evening light.

* (the process of growing old)
2/96

Old Age

Tread carefully, Helen, this is new ground.
This is not the childhood you survived
    nor the turbulent years of youth,
    not the desert places of middle age.
This is a land with new rules:
    Do not give advice, even when asked.
    Do not tell the old stories over and over.
    Do not recite your ills. They are dear only to you.
Do not ask people to speak up,
    for they are not speaking more softly than before.
    And do not ask them to repeat.
    (Not all they say is worth repeating.)
Be cheerful. Smile when they say you are exceptional.
Accept the arm that is offered,
    the best seat reserved for you,
    the door held open.
Remember, you are a pioneer with a frontier to be crossed.
You are traveling with the young and
    those who would be young,
    who do not know that they will get old.
When you are alone you may talk to yourself,
    sing a few bars of Aida,
    twirl a few dance steps while the tea water boils,
    (but only if you are alone.)
Pray for grace.

10/24/02

Called Home

In a dream near dawn,
    the sun was waiting
    to spring the day.
It faintly defined the familiar room,
    outlining the four-poster bed,
    the twining ivy at the window,
    your picture on the wall.
I saw a figure standing in the doorway,
    waiting and quiet, not hurried.
I was not frightened. He was not unexpected.
He had come once before.
When he spoke, I recognized his voice,
    soft and kind, yet firm.
"It is time to go," he said.

10/4/06

Printed in the United States
130238LV00002B/4/P